JEAN RACINE's
ANDROMACHE

Translated by Eric Korn

...

Preface by Jonathan Miller

...

Afterword by Albert Bermel

ANDROMACHE

Library of Congress Cataloging-in-Publication Data

Racine, Jean, 1639-1699.
  Jean Racine's Andromache.

  (The Old Vic Theatre collection)
  Translation of Andromaque.
  Bibliography: p.
  1. Andromache (Legendary character)—Drama. I. Korn,
Eric. II. Title. III. Series.
PQ1890.A35 1988 842'.4 87-37361
ISBN 1-55784-021-5

APPLAUSE THEATRE BOOK PUBLISHERS
211 West 71st Street
New York, NY 10023

122 Kennington Rd.
London, England SE11

CONTENTS

THE DIRECTOR'S PERSPECTIVE

by Jonathan Miller

Racine's infrequent appearance on the English stage may be ascribed to our insular view of the theatre, but it may be equally attributed to the insular nature of the plays Racine wrote. No measure of exercising Racine on our stages will shape him into Shakespeare. We cannot find in Racine those rich, discursive plots, spinning out a fecundity of characters and idiosyncratic fates. Ask any actor. Racine is no Peripatetic. He observes his mark on the stage and remains anchored there as to his fate. No amount of directorial blocking will budge him from his appointed place. We will, likewise, not find Shakespeare's private mint where the bard would coin new words, would forge a new language, transacting the business of the stage with ruthless alchemy. We must forego the pleasure of his infinite invention and wit. This apparent deprivation compounded by the inevitable loss in translation does not excite the Shakespeare-trained palate for French neo-classical fare.

We are tempted to invigorate Racine's famous imperturbable stasis by relying on the grand presentational energy of his classical Greek origins. We may also yearn for a modern naturalistic axis on which to poise Racine's complexities of character. But the Greek heroes and the modern psychological profiles are equidistantly remote from Racine's terrain. His text is dourly obdurate about any foreign governments we would impose.

We find ourselves propelled instead into a literary limbo, suspended halfway between dramatic poles. Our production at the Old Vic is set in a Seventeenth Century Elsewhere, a barely habitable ruin. Andromache's ancestors towered over their mythical landscapes, but she and her contemporaries inhabit a dusty dereliction. They are like aristocrats living in exile in the Hotel Negresco in Nice. Their language, like their other prospective fortunes, has been stripped of idiosyncrasy and color. Yet this austere regime rivets us with hypnotic fascination. As we microscopically examine drop by drop their weakening of blood, the focus widens into a startlingly telescopic vista, bringing into stark relief a historical parade of degeneration. Individuals move in morbid rotation, for the most part, in the public galaxy of duty and honor. Tragedy erupts through this Cartesian geometry only when an aberrant force, Love, passionately strains the conventional axes with its eccentric initiatives and threatens to sabotage the system.

Static? What could be less static or more spectacular than the perpetual tug-of-war between man and the solar system he futilely attempts to wrestle to the ground.

London
December, 1987

ANDROMACHE

CHARACTERS

ANDROMACHE, Hector's widow, captive of Pyrrhus

PYRRHUS, Achilles' son, King of Epirus

ORESTES, Agamemnon's son

HERMIONE, Helen's daughter, betrothed to Pyrrhus

PYLADES, friend of Orestes

CLEONE, Hermione's confidante

CEPHISA, Andromache's confidante

PHOENIX, counsellor of Achilles and, later, of Pyrrhus

ORESTES' FOLLOWERS

The following accentuation applies:

An´dromachē, Cle´onē, Pў´ladēs, 'Pўrrhus, Ce´phīsa,
Her´mi-onē, E´pīrus, As´tў anax, 'Phoē nix, O´rest ēs

The scene is at Buthrotum, a town in Epirus, in a chamber of
Pyrrhus' palace.

This version of ANDROMACHE was first presented by Ed Mirvish and David Mirvish at the Old Vic on January 15, 1988 with the following cast:

ANDROMACHE	Janet Suzman
PYRRHUS	Peter Eyre
ORESTES	Kevin McNally
HERMIONE	Penelope Wilton
PYLADES	Ben Onwukwe
CLEONE	Juanita Waterman
CEPHISA	Janet Henfrey
PHOENIX	John Barron

Director	Jonathan Miller
Costumes	Richard Hudson
Lighting	Davy Cunningham
Administrator	Andrew Leigh

ACT ONE
SCENE ONE

ORESTES, PYLADES

ORESTES

Well, yes. Believe me, I can really use a friend.
Perhaps my luck's begun to change.
                                        Perhaps
Fate hasn't got her knife in me so much,
Seeing she's let us meet here. Who'd have thought
I'd find you once again in this grim place,
That after six months, when I need you most,
I'd find you, large as life, at Pyrrhus' court?

PYLADES

I thank heaven for it.
                        I'd begun to think
Ever since the storm which drove our ships apart
When we had all but reached the Epirote coast,
That Fate would keep on getting in the way
And never let me get back home to Greece.
I've been so anxious for you, even wept,
Dreaming up new dangers that you might be in
And I, a useless friend, not there to share them.
I thought especially of those black moods
I've often seen you sunk in; was afraid
That an obliging fate might offer you
That Death that you so often seemed to seek.
Look at you now! No more the doom-struck wretch,
You're here in state, and with a retinue;

1

Almost as though your luck (but let's touch wood!)
Had turned round in Epirus, turned to good.

ORESTES

We can't predict what fate may have in store.
Dragged here by love for one who's never kind,
For what? For life? For death?

PYLADES
                    What? Are you still
A slave dependent on her tyrant will?
How has she mesmerized you to forget
The wretchedness you've been through, and submit
And hold your hands out, greedy for the chains,
To let Hermione torture you again?
You think that she, so iron-hard in Sparta,
Will melt here in Epirus?
                    Sir, I thought
You'd grown ashamed of all those wasted sighs
And hated her.
                    You didn't talk about her
Any more. You really had me fooled.

ORESTES
                    I had *me* fooled.
My friend, don't kick a friend who's down. I told you
From the beginning, everything I felt.
You saw me falling, saw my passion start;
I kept you posted. And when Menelaus
Resolved to give his daughter's hand to Pyrrhus,
The family's avenger, then you saw

Me wretched; dragging from sea to sea
My burdens and my miseries. To my shame
I dragged you too, and readily you came
Always at hand to save me from myself.
After much uproar, when I realised
The way she doted; how Hermione
Would throw herself at Pyrrhus, I grew mad,
Wanted to punish her, hurt her for her coldness
By putting her out of mind.

                          I made you think,
I thought myself, that I was winning through,
And all my passion turned to passionate hate;
I cursed her hardness, made light of her charms,
Defied that pretty face to do its worst,
And so I thought I'd cured myself of love;
Returned to Greece in a deceptive calm
To find a full-blown crisis had begun
And all the Princes gathered to confer.
I rushed to join them; thought that war and glory
Would give me more important things than love
To think about. I'd be myself again
And so get free. But how adroitly fate
Can move the trap, which we swerve to escape.
All about Greece a mumbled rumour runs
And threats against Pyrrhus.

                            He's disloyal, they say.
Forgetful of his oath, his kith and kin
He's bringing up at court, an enemy,
A foe to Greece, Astyanax, the son
Of Hector, and the one survivor, last
Of that long line of buried Trojan kings.
I learned then how, to save the baby prince
Andromache had done a switch, and fooled
Unfoolable Ulysses, who had wrenched

3

A changeling child out of her arms and killed it.
And Pyrrhus my rival—Pyrrhus, for whom, it seemed
Hermione's charms were exercised in vain—
Was offering heart and crown
elsewhere. Menelaus
Didn't believe it; nonetheless seemed worried
And wondered why the wedding was delayed.
Out of the troubles that so heaped on him
I filched a secret pleasure; and I gloated,
Flattering myself that all I felt was anger,
And a thirst for vengeance all I had in mind.
But that ungrateful creature in my heart
Came back to life. The still-warm ash rekindled
I felt my hate begin to die away.
No, that's a lie.
I knew I'd always loved her.
And so I lobbied all the delegations;
Won the appointment. Got the Greeks to send me
To Pyrrhus as their envoy, here to try
To tear from him the child whose very life
Threatens the peace of many kingdoms.
Passion compels me.
If I can abduct
The princess, not the child—not Astyanax,
But Hermione—then do not suppose
There's any risk I'm not prepared to run.
Since I can't cleanse this fever from my mind
I accept my fate. I'll follow, abject, blind.
I've come to find Hermione: she's the prize
I'll win and carry off; or die before her eyes.
You know Pyrrhus: tell me how things set,
What goes on in his head and in his cabinet
And with Hermione; does she still hold sway
Or will he give back what he stole away?

PYLADES

I should deceive you Sir to let you think
That Pyrrhus was about to let her go
Even though he gets no joy from having won her.
His passion now is for Andromache
Who gives him the cold shoulder: and each day
He tries new tricks to sway her or to scare her,
Threatens to kill her son, whom he's got hidden,
Reduces her to tears, then comforts her;
Goes back to Hermione, makes his peace with her,
Renews his promises, and falling at her feet
Raves, less from love than anger; don't expect
Me to predict what that wild heart may do.
He's liable, in his disordered state,
To wound what he loves; to marry out of hate.

ORESTES

And Hermione? How does she feel to find
The wedding day postponed, her hold
On Pyrrhus broken?

PYLADES

                    Publicly, at least,
She treats his vacillations with contempt,
Seems confident that he'll come back to heel.
But I've seen her in private, hurt to tears
At his behaviour: on the point of leaving
But still staying on: and more than once or twice
I've heard her wish Orestes here to help.

ORESTES

If I thought, Pylades, that that was true
I'd fling myself . . .

PYLADES
                                No flinging, Sir! Your message
Must be delivered. King Pyrrhus made to see
How Hector's son unites all Greece against him:
Then there's no risk the boy will be surrendered.
Their anger will just strengthen his resolve
And make him love Andromache the more.
The more you try to stir things up between them
The more he'll cling to her. You must demand
The maximum, to be sure of getting nothing.
Here he comes.

ORESTES
                            Then you must go to her
And warn that cruel woman that I'm here;
That I'm here just to see her.

SCENE TWO

PYRRHUS, ORESTES, PHOENIX

ORESTES

I come to you to speak for all the Greeks,
Princes confederate who have formed a league;
But let me tell you first how proud I am
To represent them.
                          Sent to greet you here
Achilles' son, the conqueror of Troy.
The father brought Prince Hector tumbling down
His son with equal daring took his town.
True son to a true Greek.
                          But now you plan
To do what he would not; what all of Greece
Deplores: you are rearming Troy
And with a misplaced pity you preserve
The war's last remnant. Think who Hector was;
How Greece, still bleeding, trembles at his name.
Our widows and our orphans can't forget him.
There's not a household in the whole of Greece
But Hector's son owes blood to:
                          fathers, husbands.
That son, grown up, might turn his hand to . . . think
Of ports assaulted, our fleets burnt at anchor
Or driven out to sea by threats of flame.
With your permission, I'll be entirely frank:
You yourself, Sir, would do well to fear.
The snake you foster may yet turn on you
And punish you for saving him.
                          Give
The Greeks their due. Take vengeance. Guard yourself.

7

Uproot an enemy the more dangerous
Because Epirus represents to him
A dress rehearsal for his Greek campaign.

PYRRHUS

I had imagined some emergency
Preoccupied the Heads of State of Greece
Who send you here as their ambassador,
Of some grand project.
                                    I'm touched that they should show
So much anxiety on my behalf;
And send the son of noble Agamemnon
As special envoy from the Greeks in Council:
A whole victorious nation met in Congress
To plot the murder of a Trojan toddler!
Why must I sacrifice him? To what God?
Why do the Greeks have any claim on him?
Or why am I less free than other generals
To dispose of all my captives as I please?
When, underneath the smoking walls of Troy
The bloody victors parcelled out the loot
By drawing lots, I drew Andromache
Together with her son. And random chance
Allotted Hecuba to Ulysses,
Cassandra to your father: have I sought
Consultatory rights about *their* fate
Or stuck my oar in?
                                    Hector's son a danger?
Might be the founder of a second Troy?
Might take my life, because I let him live?
You carry caution to extremes, my Lord;
The danger's too remote to fret about
And I'm not given to meeting trouble halfway.

8

I can still see that City as it was
Its proud walls and its towers, hosts of heroes,
Mistress of Asia. All that glory vanished,
Its towers heaps of rubble; cinders, ashes,
A river stained with blood, abandoned fields,
A child in chains . . . is this a State
Bent upon vengeance?
                                    This child's death
Was sworn, you claim? Then why was it postponed
For twelve months until now? Why was he not
Slaughtered along with Priam in the ruins?
One death, among so many?
                                    Fair enough:
For neither age nor innocence were spared
Night and the lust of victory made us savage;
We killed like blundering butchers, I as much as anyone,
Was brutal to the losers.
                                    But to go on,
Continue killing with the rage burnt out
And murder in cold blood? Suppress my pity,
And liquidate this infant at my leisure?
The Greeks must find themselves another target
Or carry their vendetta somewhere else.
Epirus will protect what's left of Troy.

ORESTES

Who was the mastermind behind the trick
To substitute a fake Astyanax
And send him to the execution place
Where only Hector's son would fit the bill?
It isn't Troy, but Hector we pursue;
The Greeks owe him a debt of too much blood
Which only blood will cancel out: a debt

9

They'll come to settle even in Epirus
Unless you can forestall them.

PYRRHUS
Let them come.
Let them start here a second Trojan War,
And welcome, if they're blinded by their hate
So that they don't discriminate between
The blood of victor or the blood of victim.
It's not the first time they have been unjust
In paying off the debt they owed Achilles.
The last occasion, Hector gained by it;
Perhaps, this time his son may benefit.

ORESTES
Must I report that you are still rebellious?

PYRRHUS
Report I said I didn't win their war
To be their errand boy.

ORESTES
Hermione
Must make the peace between her father and you
You won't ignore her.

PYRRHUS
No, Hermione
Will always be extremely dear to me,

10

Which doesn't mean I'll be her father's slave.
And one day I may manage to balance out
The claims of Prestige and the claims of Love.
Meanwhile I know that you and she are close,
Close kin.
    I give you leave to speak with her.
Thereafter Sir, I won't detain you longer;
Your mission's over, you are free to go
And tell the Greek my answer:
        which is 'No.'

SCENE THREE

PYRRHUS, PHOENIX

PHOENIX

And so . . . you've sent him off to his beloved?

PYRRHUS

They say that he's been after her for years.

PHOENIX

It's been known
     for old flames to blaze up afresh. Suppose
He makes a play for her again, and wins her?

PYRRHUS
If they become a couple—fine by me!
If they swan off, all starry-eyed, to Sparta
Taking my problems with them:
                                    'There's the boat
Please don't let me detain you.'

PHOENIX
Sir . . .

PYRRHUS
        Another time I'll tell what's on my mind
Here comes Andromache.

SCENE FOUR

PYRRHUS, ANDROMACHE, CEPHISA

PYRRHUS
                Is it me
You're looking for? Or do I fool myself?

ANDROMACHE
I'm on my way to where they keep my son.
The single daily visit you permit
Is all I've left of Hector and of Troy,
We'll cry for them together.
                        I've not given him, Sir,
His daily hug.

PYRRHUS
If the Greeks have their way
Then you'll have more to cry for.

ANDROMACHE
                              What's the bogey
They're so afraid of? Is there a Trojan left?

PYRRHUS
Their phobia about Hector still runs deep:
They fear his son.

ANDROMACHE
                    And well they might!
A wretched child who doesn't understand
His father's dead, and he's in Pyrrhus' hands.

PYRRHUS
Whatever he may be, they want him dead.
Orestes has been sent to speed the process.

ANDROMACHE
And will you sign so barbarous an order?
Is it my caring makes him seem a menace?
They're not afraid that he'll come seeking vengeance;
It's just that he's a comfort to his mother
That makes them hate him. He could fill the gap
Left by my father, and my husband.
                                    No;
I must lose all I have, and all through you.

13

PYRRHUS

No need for tears. Madam, I've turned them down.
Greece has already threatened me with war.
But even if they should come sailing here,
The thousand ships put out to sea again
To spill as much blood as your Hector spilt;
If I must stand another ten-year siege
And see my town in ashes: even then
I would not waver; I'd rush headlong in
And jeopardize my life to save your son's.
I'm risking all I am to try and please you:
Just for a friendly glance.
                              On every side
My enemies harrass me. Must I fight
Against you too, when I might be your friend?
I'm offering to be your strength.
                              Will you consent
To let me be your lover? Will you take
A heart that worships?
                              If I fight for you
Can I delete you from my list of foes?

ANDROMACHE

What do you mean to do?
                              And how will Greece interpret it?
Why must a hero seem so feeble-hearted?
Do you want this grand design to seem to them
The ravings of a love-besotted fool?
Captive, in mourning, a burden to myself
Can you expect Andromache to love you?
What do you see in me? What special charm
To see me weeping for the pain you've caused me?
At least respect a fallen enemy;

14

Be merciful and give me back my son,
Fight off the enemies that encircle us,
But do not ask my love. Save him
Even in spite of me. That would be a gesture
Well worthy of Achilles' noble son.

PYRRHUS

Must you remain my enemy for ever?
Is there no end to hatred or to blame?
Well, I deserve it.

            I fought against your country,
I've killed my share of Trojans; more than my share.
I'm paying for it now

            with more than my share of trouble.
All that we did to Troy

          you've done to me.
Defeated and enslaved, in chains, bereaved
and burnt, burnt with Greek fire,

          burnt by fiercer flames
Than any that I lit.

         I never was
As merciless to Troy as you to me.
It's time to put a period to my sentence,
Time we had more than enemies in common.
If only you will tell me I've a chance
I'll give you back your son, I'll be his father,
I'll learn to share your Trojan sense of wrong,
Punish the Greeks for what they've done to us
And—with your blessing—try to rebuild Troy;
Then in less time than the Greeks fought to take it,
Raise up those walls; and on them, crown your son.

15

ANDROMACHE

Your grandiose designs no longer move me.
I had designs like those, while Hector lived;
I've no ambition now to see those walls
Those fine defenses that could not shield Hector.
My hope's more modest; just to live in peace
Away from Troy, away from Greeks, and you;
To shelter with my son and be a widow.
Your love for me provokes my enemies
Go back to her.
                    Go back to Helen's daughter.
Back to Hermione.

PYRRHUS

                    How could I? Don't torment me.
How can I give my heart when you possess it?
I know I offered her my fealty,
And she is here to govern in Epirus.
Fate sent you both. You to wear chains
                                        and she
To forge chains for me. I've not tried to please her
And anyone would say, who saw you both,
You overwhelming me, her left to mope,
That she's the captive here, and you are Queen.
Ah! If I fired off in her direction
A single one of all the pretty speeches
I aim at you, how grateful she would be!

ANDROMACHE

Why would she be ungrateful? She can count
The glorious deeds you've done.
                                Troy demolished

And Hector slaughtered; these don't sicken her,
She doesn't have to mourn a husband dead
And such a husband!
                    Unendurable!
It's only Hector's death that brought your father
Immortal fame. He owes it all to him.
The reputation that you both enjoy
Is founded on my tears.

PYRRHUS
                    That's it then, lady.
I must forget you; rather, I must hate you,
Because my passion has driven me too far
To settle for indifference.
                    Bear in mind
That either I adore you or I loathe you.
I'll revel in my anger, sparing no-one.
You've hurt me, and your son will pay for it.
The Greeks demand his head;
                              why should I put
My kingdom on the line when you're not grateful
For what I'd risk to save you?

ANDROMACHE
                    Then he dies!
He only has his mother's tears to save him, that
And his innocence. These don't count for much.
Perhaps I'm better off. When he is gone
I'm that much closer to the end of grief,
Since he is all I live for.
                    Afterwards
I'll follow him and go to meet his father.

Then through your care, we three will be together,
I thank you for our . . .

PYRRHUS
                    Go and see your son.
Perhaps a gentler kind of mother-love
Will make you see that anger isn't always
The surest guide to action.
                              I'll come to you
Shortly, to learn what fate you plan for us.
So while you hug him, think of ways to save him.

ACT TWO
SCENE ONE

HERMIONE, CLEONE

HERMIONE

I'll do what you suggest: I'll let him see me
Since he wants it so much, I'll give him that;
He's due here soon with Pylades;

                    if I trusted
To my own instincts, I'd not let him near.

CLEONE

Why will it be so hard? He's still Orestes,
That same Orestes you have wished was back
A hundred times; whose love and constancy
You've a hundred times regretted.

HERMIONE

I didn't value—then—his constancy;
Now I'm ashamed to face him: what a triumph
For him;

         for me, humiliation!
Now it's my turn to suffer. 'What, can that be her?'
—he'll say—'Is that the proud Hermione
The one who snubbed me? Turn and turn about;
She put so high a value on her love
And now loves one who scorns it: serve her right!
She'll find out how it feels to be despised!'
O God . . .

19

CLEONE
This fear's unworthy.
You think your lover's coming here to crow?
He's too much in your power: brings a heart
He never could take from you.
                              You've not told me:
What were your father's orders?

HERMIONE
If Pyrrhus keeps delaying, won't consent
To Special Handling for the Trojan brat
His orders are I leave here with the Greeks.

CLEONE
You'd best attend to what Orestes says.
Pyrrhus has made the break—or started to—
And you must finish—since you say you hate him.

HERMIONE
Hate him! It's my honour that's at stake:
The sweet attentions which are now forgotten,
So dear to me, and now so treacherous,
I loved him too much not to hate him now.

CLEONE
Then quit him, madam: and since there's one who loves you . . .

HERMIONE

Allow my anger time and room to grow;
Let me convince myself how much I hate him
The cheat has done his work too well, Cleone;
I'm sick at heart at leaving.

CLEONE

                              You'd prefer
To wait for some new insult? Not content
To see him love his prisoner, watch him woo her
In front of you; isn't that sufficient
To make him loathsome to you? If it's not,
I can't suggest what else he ought to try.
You'd hate him now, it hate were possible.

HERMIONE

Why try to make me feel worse? I don't dare
Inspect my feelings in my present state.
Don't believe what you see, or try not to.
Believe I hate him, believe my heart is hardened,
Believe there's nothing left in it but scorn,
Congratulate me on my self-control;
Believe in it.
                    Please.
                              Make me believe it too.
You think I ought to run away from him?
What's stopping me? Envy of that captive,
Who's captured him? But suppose the twister
Had second thoughts, recalled his obligations
And came and begged forgiveness? Suppose
Love brought him back to heel . . .
                                        He only wants

To trample me. I'll stay, just to be awkward;
I'll take my pleasure out of spoiling theirs.
I'll make him breach his promise publicly,
His solemn vows; so that the Greeks denounce him.
Just as I've stirred their rage against the son,
So let the mother's life be forfeit. Let her suffer
As I have been tortured. Let his passion bring
Ruin to her or let her ruin him.

CLEONE

Do you think those eyes for ever blind with tears
Sparkle with simple pleasure at the thought
That your attractions don't match up to hers?
Or that that heart so busy with its sorrows
Craves the attentions of the very man
Who caused those sorrows? Think that she's consoled
Or cares if Pyrrhus fancies her?
                              Think she looks
The happier for it?
                    If so, why the tears?
And if his love was welcome, why behave
Towards the lover with such hostility?

HERMIONE

I wasn't hostile.
                  And now I'm paying for it.
I didn't play at being the silent type
But thought that I could safely speak my mind
Without a moment's caution or reserve.
I told him all of what was in my heart
And wouldn't anyone have trusted him
After the vows he swore?

                            Did he see me
Then, as he sees me now?
                            Remember
How everything conspired in his favour:
My family avenged, the Greeks triumphant,
Our troopships homeward bound, weighed down with loot
And how his score of victories
Eclipsed his father's, and—so it appeared—
His love for me more passionate
                                        than mine for him:
And even you, my dear, so thrilled by him,
You all betrayed me, long before he did.
Enough's enough: whatever Pyrrhus was
He is no longer; I'm not stone, I see
The merits of Orestes: he can love at least
And love with return: perhaps he knows
The way to make me love him.
                                        Let him come.

CLEONE

Madam, he's here.

HERMIONE

I didn't think that he would be so near.

SCENE TWO

HERMIONE, ORESTES, CLEONE

HERMIONE

Should I believe some tenderness remains,
You pity me, a little?
                            Or is it duty
That brings you here so promptly?

ORESTES

See how love's blinded me; you know my fate:
To keep on falling at your feet, to worship you
And then to swear it's finished. And I know
One glance from you, and old wounds open up;
My resolution crumbles every time;
My promises are straw.
                            I blush for it, God knows,
But God's my witness, God who saw me raving
When last I left you, how I tried to die
And rushed to every place where death seemed sure
To free me from my vows and from your chains.
I begged for death from certain savage tribes
Who fed their gods on human blood: but they
Rejected me and shut their temple doors;
The bloodthirsty turned squeamish.
So I'm here. Give me the look that kills.
Forbid me hope. Tell me one more time
What you have said so often. That'll do
My business for me. For the last long year
That's all I've looked for. Say the word

And take that scalp the Scythians would have had
Were they as cruel as you.

HERMIONE

Orestes, stop this self-indulgent talk.
Greece has a job for you. Stop chattering
Of Scythians, or of how cruel I am.
Think of the kings whose embassy you bear;
Must their high vengeance hang upon your mood?
Have you been asked to sacrifice your life
Or carry out the mission you've been set?

ORESTES

Pyrrhus rejects my case; my mission's done,
I'm turned away; some force beyond himself
Makes him give Hector's son his full protection.

HERMIONE

The traitor!

ORESTES

                    So, all prepared to leave,
I came to speak to you about my fate;
Although I can hear already, in my head,
The cold reply you'd like to give to me.

HERMIONE

Where is this coldness you profess to see
In your unending and unjust complaint?

25

Am I the cruel person that you claim?
I came to Epirus, as my father ordered
A dutiful daughter: but what makes you sure
I didn't share your grief?

                    Are you alone
In suffering? Haven't I wept too, in secret?
What makes you think I didn't chafe at duty
Sometimes, and long to see you?

ORESTES
                  To see me?
Princess, is this me you're talking to?
Take a look: it's me. Orestes.

              Me,
That makes you sick to look at.

HERMIONE
            You,
Whose love for me first made me realise
The power that lay within me: you
Whom now I start to learn to value, you
My heart goes out to; you I'd wish to love.

ORESTES
I understand. I get the beggar's part
For me—your best wishes.

                  Pyrrhus has your heart.

HERMIONE
Don't envy Pyrrhus. I'd hate you too much . . .

ORESTES

Yes. But love me more!

You look at me with such ambiguous eyes
You'd love to love me but I cannot please you.
Love won't appear to order: you'd do better
To try to hate me: that might make love grow.
And I could offer you so much, such understanding
Proper respect, to treat you with such care
As you deserve: if only you could listen
As I must listen to this talk of Pyrrhus
Despite yourself, perhaps; in spite of him,
Certainly. He just despises you
You know he's set his heart on someone else . . .

HERMIONE

And what makes you imagine
That he despises me?

Do his words, his looks

Give that impression to you? Am I then
Despicable? Someone to love and tire of?

Others

May find me less forgettable than you do.

ORESTES

Encore! Encore! Insult me if you like;
I'm not the lover that despises you.
Haven't you gathered yet that you can trust me?
Do I show signs of getting tired of you,
Forgetting ?. . .

Won't you realise

That he's the one resistant to your charms?

HERMIONE

His love, his scorn: they're all the same to me.
He is a traitor. Let him suffer for it
The punishment of traitors.
                              Raise the Greeks;
Mobilise armies to destroy Epirus,
And let it burn like Troy.
                              On your way!
Now will you claim I love him?

ORESTES

                              Then do more:
Come away with me, help persuade the Council.
For you could sway them. Why stay here a hostage?

HERMIONE

But then Andromache will marry him.

ORESTES

But . . .

HERMIONE

        Think of the insult to our national honour
If he were married to a Phrygian!

ORESTES

Is this the way you hate him?
                              O admit
You can't turn love off like a water tap.

Your looks, your words, your silences betray you
And it will flood out somewhere!

HERMIONE

It's no use arguing. Your mind's quite closed.
You turn my words against me, twist
And poison what I say, even think hatred
Is just love in disguise. I'll say it plainly,
And then you're bound to act.
                                        It's only duty
Towards my father brought me to this place
And duty keeps me here, and I must stay
Till Pyrrhus or my father lets me go.
You go to Pyrrhus, you explain to him,
As coming from my father, that a rebel
Is no fit son-in-law.
                            So he must choose
Between the Trojan child and me.
                                        He cannot keep
The two of us; must either send me off
Or hand him over. So, for now, goodbye.
I'll leave with you, if he gives his consent.

SCENE THREE

ORESTES, *alone*

ORESTES
Yes, you'll go with me. Now I'm sure of it.
I guarantee that he'll make no objection
For he's besotted with his Trojan woman,
Has only eyes for her. You're in his way
And he'll be glad to get you off his hands
On any pretext.
                    Just a word with him
Will do the trick. What a joy for me
To steal so choice a trophy from Epirus.
Let him preserve these last remains of Troy,
Keep Hector's wife, his son, a thousand more
For all I care.
                    Hermione
Has seen the last of Pyrrhus and his land.
But by some chance, here comes the man himself!
I'll talk to him.
                    Then, God of Love, be kind:
To her attractions let him still be blind.

SCENE FOUR

PYRRHUS, ORESTES, PHOENIX

PYRRHUS

I came to find you. Perhaps I was too brusque
In countering your arguments. They have some force,
I grant you; and thinking over things
It seems to me you've justice on your side.
I'm going against Greece, against my father
Against myself, if I help rebuild Troy
Undoing all we fought for,
                                        Achilles and myself;
I think your grievance is legitimate.
The boy will be surrendered.

ORESTES

A very bold and statesmanlike decision!
A child's blood to make our peace secure.

PYRRHUS

Yes, and I'll make it even more secure.
Hermione shall be the pledge of peace:
I'm marrying her; and you shall be the witness
To this auspicious rite: you shall be
The representative of all of Greece
And of her father. Menelaus sees
His brother brought to life again in you.
Go call on her. Go now. Tell her, tomorrow,
I count on you to give the bride away,
And with her, peace.

31

ORESTES
God. O God. O God.

SCENE FIVE

PYRRHUS, PHOENIX

PYRRHUS
What do you think, Phoenix; does love still master me?
Am I myself again?

PHOENIX
                    Indeed, you are Sir,
And your just anger—with pressure from the Greeks—
Has brought you round and made you sensible.
No longer passion's plaything but yourself,
Achilles' son and equal.
                    Your self-respect
Has made you take a step you can be proud of
And Troy has fallen for the second time.

PYRRHUS
It's more like—that my victory over Troy
Has just begun; and now I can enjoy it.
My heart's my own again! That makes me proud
As if I'd beaten a whole regiment.
Think of the problems that I'm free of now,

32

And all the troubles love brings in its wake:
The sacrifice of duty and of power
The dangers . . . all forgotten for a glance!
The Greeks as one man would have piled on me
And gladly I'd have wrecked myself for her.

PHOENIX

Thank Heavens you got tough with her in time!

PYRRHUS

You were a witness how she treated me.
Seeing her tenderness toward her son
I thought I could get close to her through him.
But all I got was tears, was angry tears
Relieved by intervals of hysteria.
Suffering made her bitter. Every day
She talked of Hector, Hector all the time.
I offered my protection: it did no good.
'It's Hector!' says she, kissing the child some more,
'His very eyes, his mouth; already bold, like him . . .
It's you, my husband.'
                                        Did the woman think
That I had saved Astyanax to be
A sort of shrine to Hector?

PHOENIX

That might be what she had in store for you
But let's forget her.

PYRRHUS
I know how she went wrong:
By banking on her beauty. I grew angry
But still she thought I'd grovel at her feet.
She'll grovel at mine and I won't give a damn.
She's Hector's widow?
                          I'm Achilles' son.
There's too much hate between us.

PHOENIX
It's time to start to talk about her less
Go to Hermione: work at pleasing her,
To take your mind off your discomfiture.
It's you must coax her to the wedding-place;
Don't leave it to your rival to do that
He still loves her too much.

PYRRHUS
                          Do you suppose
Deep down, Andromache will feel jealousy
When I get married?

PHOENIX
                          What difference does it make
To you if she is delighted or downcast?
Can you not think of any other topic?
What is this magic spell she's cast on you?

PYRRHUS

I didn't tell her all I need to say;
She doesn't know the half of how I hate her.
We'll go to her; I'll look her in the eye
And let my anger rip.
                        You'll see
She'll get what she deserves.

PHOENIX
                        Go
Crawl at her feet and tell her you adore her
Encourage her to sneer at you some more.

PYRRHUS

You think that I'm still ready to forgive
And look for ways to make my peace with her?

PHOENIX

You're still in love, that's all.

PYRRHUS
                        Me, in love
With one who hates me more, the more I try
To soften her? No family or friends
And no one to support her, except me;
I could have her son killed, I should perhaps . . .
An alien . . . no, a slave here in Epirus!
I offer her her son, my throne, myself
And that ungrateful slut looks down on me
As her chief torturer? I'm resolute

For once she'll have some real cause to hate me.
Her son must go.
                              Oh, there'll be tears!
The names she'll find to call me.
                                        What a scene
I'm setting up for her.
                              She'll die of it.
It'll kill her, Phoenix, and I'll be the cause
As if I thrust a dagger in her heart.

PHOENIX

But why risk having everything go wrong
By making no allowance for your weakness?

PYRRHUS

I take your point. I'm not as weak as that;
There's just a remnant of my tenderness
A dying love's last gasp.
                              Let's go along
I'll trust your judgement, Phoenix.
                                        Must her son
Be handed over? Must I go and see
                              Hermione?

PHOENIX

You must, Sir. And with your solemn word
Persuade her . . .

PYRRHUS
What I've sworn, I'll do.

ACT THREE
SCENE ONE

ORESTES, PYLADES

PYLADES
Orestes, you are raving; calm yourself
I hardly know you.
                    You're beside yourself
If I may say so . . .

ORESTES
                    No, you have said too much
I'm sick of listening to good advice
On how to best drag out this bastard life.
For I must kidnap her, or I must die.
The plan's worked out and now it's time for action:
That's what I want.

PYLADES
                    She has to be abducted, I agree;
And in the meantime, you must bear in mind
Whose country you are in.
                    What will they think
To see how you go on?
                    They'll grow suspicious.
Put on a poker face:
                    this court, these guards
The very air we breathe
                    belongs to Pyrrhus;

Hermione most of all
                    mustn't see your anger:
What possessed you
                    to come and see her in this frame of mind?

ORESTES

How can I tell you? Did it look as though
I knew what I was doing?
                         I was wild
With fury and perhaps I had in mind
A confrontation with the two of them.
                                        With
The bitch and with her lover.

PYLADES

What good would that have done?

ORESTES

But wouldn't anyone feel desperate
After a blow like that?
                        They're going to marry
Tomorrow, Pyrrhus and Hermione,
And he wants me to give the bride away
To honour me.
              I'd rather give him this . . .

PYLADES

You're blaming Pyrrhus for the freaks of fate,
But he's tormented by his own obsessions;
Perhaps he's to be pitied
                          as much as you.

38

ORESTES

O no, I know him. He sees my despair
And it amuses him.
                    If he didn't know
I loved Hermione, he'd look down on her.
He's been indifferent to her up till now:
He claims her just to spite me.
                              Gods!
It was all settled.
                    Hermione was won over
And she would never cross his path again;
Still hesitant between disgust and love,
She only needed one rejection more
To make her mine. She'd woken, Pylades
Could see Orestes as he was at last,
Talked to me, cared for me.
                              It only needed
One word to do the trick.

PYLADES
                    Do you believe that?

ORESTES

We both saw it.
How furiously she raged at his deceit . . .

PYLADES

She never loved him more than at that moment.
If Pyrrhus had delivered her to you
She would have found some pretext for delay,
Believe me.

Haven't you had enough
Of all her cheats and charms? Instead of plotting
This kidnap, you should plan to run away.
For good.
                    Or would you rather tie yourself
To an avenging fury who will hate you
Your whole life long, eternally resentful
And wistful for the man she might have had?

ORESTES

But that is why I mean to kidnap her!
Or do you reckon, Pylades, I should leave,
When everything smiles on her; and for my share
Carry away my bottled, useless rage
To travel in foreign parts, try to forget?
No! I want her to share my wretchedness;
Misery loves company. I'm sick of being pitied
I want her to be terrified of me. I want her tears
To wallow in. I want to hear her curse me
With every foul name that I've put on her.

PYLADES

There's a fine outcome of your embassy:
Orestes, rapist.

ORESTES

Pylades, so what?
Although the States were pleased they'd been avenged
She'd be more pleased, seeing me in pain.
The gratitude of Greece will leave me cold
If in Epirus I'm a laughingstock. And frankly

I'm sick of always being the injured party,
The innocent one.
                  Whatever unjust God
Punishes innocence and leaves crime alone,
The evils that he's heaped on me cry out
To heaven for justice.
                  If the Gods hate me
I'll give them reason for it.
                      Let me enjoy the crime
Before the punishment.
                  But as for you
How did you end up in the line of fire?
I am the target.
                You have been my friend
Too long, and suffer for it. Leave me here
And wash your hands of one you cannot help
Pity has warped your judgement.
                      Leave me be:
The consequences of my acts are mine.
And I must bear them.
                Take charge of the child
When Pyrrhus shall surrender him to me,
And then get going.

PYLADES
We'll take Hermione
Courage will guide us through the worst of dangers;
Where love and friendship can cooperate
There's nothing they can't do. Get all your Greeks
Together, fire up their enthusiasm,
The ships are ready and the wind is right.
I know the backdoor ways about the palace;
The sea breaks on the castle wall in places,

By night we'll have no trouble creeping out
By secret passageways towards our ships
Bringing our prize with us.

ORESTES

You're too long-suffering, and I take advantage:
Forgive me for these wrongs that only you
Could pardon.
           Find excuses for a wretch
Who wrecks the life of everyone he cares for,
Who's hated by the world, who hates himself.
If things were different I could pay you back . . .

PYLADES

Just hide your feelings, Sir, that's all I ask
Don't let our plans slip out before we strike;
Till then, forget Hermione betrays you,
Forget your love . . .
           Who is approaching.

ORESTES
           Go.
If you can be responsible for her,
           I'll answer for myself.

SCENE TWO

HERMIONE, ORESTES, CLEONE

ORESTES

You've got your wandering lover back again,
And thanks to me. I had a talk with Pyrrhus
The wedding's on again.

HERMIONE

They tell me so;
And told me, furthermore,
That you were only coming to inform me.

ORESTES

In your heart of hearts
Is there no smidgeon of rebelliousness?

HERMIONE

Who would have thought he loved me all along?
That he'd come back, at the eleventh hour,
When I'd resolved to leave him?
I fear to think—as you do—that it's the Greeks
That he defers to. That it's politics,
Not passion moves him.
That you love me most.

ORESTES

Hermione, he loves you. There's no doubt.
You can win anyone you set your mind to.
You obviously don't want to turn him down.

HERMIONE

How could I? I am bound by solemn vows.
It's not for me to snatch away a gift
That others gave him.
                          I am a princess
Not free to love according to my will.
Obedience is our glory. But remember
That I was ready to go off with you
And to forget my duty.

ORESTES

                          You'd forgotten
Nothing. But we are free to call our souls our own;
And yours is in your gift. I had some hope,
But in the end you had the right to give it;
You didn't rob me.
                          Destiny's to blame.
Not you. You must be bored by my complaining.
You've done your duty.
                          Now I must do mine.
And spare you listening to this tedious whine.

SCENE THREE

HERMIONE, CLEONE

HERMIONE

I never thought he'd be lukewarm in anger.

                              Did you, Cleone?

CLEONE

Still waters, Madam. I grieve for him, I do;
The more so since he brought it on himself:
He set the mine that blew his hopes apart.
This wedding has long been vaguely on its way:
He speaks his piece and Pyrrhus names the day.

HERMIONE

You think that Pyrrhus is afraid? Of what?
That mob that ran from Hector for ten years
And every time Achilles turned his back
Ran to their ships for cover?

                              People who
Without Achilles' son to help them fight,
Would still be trying to get their Helen back
By asking nicely? No, Cleone, no.
Pyrrhus is his own man: if he weds me, he wants me.
Orestes may lay all his woes on me,
We've better things to talk of.

                              Pyrrhus
Has come back to me. Cleone, Cleone
Can't you imagine how I'm feeling, see

45

What kind of man he is, the things he's done—
But who can count the great things he has done?
He's fearless, a born winner; he has charm
And I can trust him: what more could you ask?
Just think . . .

CLEONE
Just hush; and don't display your feelings
Here comes your rival. Shortly she'll be kneeling
Down at your feet or crying on your shoulder.

HERMIONE
Lord, can't I be left to revel in my joy;
What can I tell her? Cleone, let's go.

SCENE FOUR

ANDROMACHE, CEPHISA, HERMIONE, CLEONE

ANDROMACHE
You're off somewhere?
Doesn't it do your heart good to see me,
Great Hector's widow, blubbering at your feet?
I've not come here to make a jealous scene
Because your charms have stolen Pyrrhus' heart.
There only was one heart my heart went out to:
I watched a lance go through it.

46

Hector woke my heart;
                    it's buried with him.
I've one thing left. My son. One day you'll know
What mother love is; but you won't ever
(At least I hope you won't) be forced to know
How far a mother's love will make her go,
When mother love is all that she's got left
Of all her bright possessions.
                                When,
After ten years of war, the shell-shocked Trojans
Were ready to take vengeance on your mother
I spoke to Hector and his backing saved her.
Can't you work the same miracle with Pyrrhus?
Why are they frightened of this shipwrecked child?
We'll find some empty island for ourselves
Where he can grow up in his mother's care,
My only care to teach him how to weep.

HERMIONE
I sympathise; but I'm not free to act.
I dare not go against my father's wish;
And I must do my duty as his daughter:
It is his will that drives on Pyrrhus' rage.
If anyone can move him, then it's you;
He was your slave for so long.
                                Get his support
I'll second him.

SCENE FIVE

ANDROMACHE, CEPHISA

ANDROMACHE
She's hard . . .
You saw with what contempt she turned me down!

CEPHISA
But do as she advises: talk to Pyrrhus
One look from you can ruin her and Greece.
And here he comes, to find you.

SCENE SIX

PYRRHUS, ANDROMACHE, PHOENIX, CEPHISA

PYRRHUS
                                    Where's the Princess?
I thought you said I'd find her hereabouts.

PHOENIX
I thought so.

ANDROMACHE
(to CEPHISA)
One look and he comes running!

PYRRHUS
What's she saying, Phoenix?

ANDROMACHE
I've lost it all!

PHOENIX
Come on, let's find Hermione.

CEPHISA
What are you waiting for? Say something to him.

ANDROMACHE
He promised me my son.

CEPHISA
But he's still got him.

ANDROMACHE
What use my crying? He's as good as dead.

PYRRHUS
Is she too proud even to look at us
Too high-and-mighty?

ANDROMACHE
I'll only make him angrier.
Let's go.

PYRRHUS
Let's go.
And give Astyanax up to the Greeks.

ANDROMACHE
O stop my Lord. What do you mean to do?
If you surrender him, surrender me!
You promised so much love: is nothing left
Not even pity? Is there no appeal?

PYRRHUS
Phoenix will tell you—I have given my word.

ANDROMACHE
You offered to take on the world for me.

PYRRHUS
I was blind; but now my eyes are opened.
I would have granted everything you asked;
You would not ask.
And now it's settled.

ANDROMACHE

King, Majesty, you surely understand
My fear of being rejected? Then forgive
The scrap of pride that's all that's left to me
Of my high rank; that is ashamed to beg.
I could not kneel to any man but you.

PYRRHUS

I know you hate me: deep down, you're afraid
Of any obligation to my love.
That son you cherish, if I gave him to you
You'd turn against him. You hate me and despise me
More than all the Greeks together.

        Take your noble rage

And stew in it. Phoenix!

ANDROMACHE

     I must go

And join my husband.

CEPHISA

     Madam, try again . . .

ANDROMACHE

There isn't any more that I can say.
Since he's the one brought all my troubles on me
Do you suppose he doesn't know what they are?
     (To PYRRHUS*)*
Sir, this is the state that you have brought me to:
I've seen my father dead, and Troy's walls burning,

51

My family slaughtered, and my husband Hector
Dragged through the bloody dust. And Hector's son,
My son, with me, destined to be a slave.
But a child brings Hope. I lived, I slaved, for him;
And I did more. Sometimes I thanked my fate
That I was exiled here and nowhere else
And that my son was lucky in his misfortune
That he, the son of many sons of kings
Was here your servant, that his prison
Might be a sort of haven. Since Achilles
Had shown the humbled Priam such respect
(When he came begging for the corpse of Hector)
I thought his son would be as merciful.
Hector, forgive me for my innocence;
I did not dream your enemy was ignoble:
I thought he might be generous
                                                    —just enough
To leave us at the tomb I built for you,
And end his hate there, let me end my life,
And there with Hector bury Hector's wife.

PYRRHUS

Wait, till I send for you, Phoenix.

SCENE SEVEN

PYRRHUS, ANDROMACHE, CEPHISA

PYRRHUS
Lady, please.
This mourning for your son is premature.
I know I have made you cry: I'm sorry for it.
I've given you cause to hate me.
Listen;
Look at me at least: do I have the face
Of a hanging judge, who's trying to do you harm?
Then why do you force me to act against you?
For your son's sake, let's stop this quarrelling.
I want to save him:
Do I have to beg?
Do you insist I grovel in the dirt?
For the last time,
save him.
Save me.
I gave my word: I'm breaking it for you;
How they will hate me!
Hermione
Sent packing. Not with the crown she came for
But the order of the boot. The temple
All flower-bedecked for her, I'll bring you to;
Tie round your head
the garland meant for her.
My final offer: imperial power or ruin;
A year of loving you without return
Has made me crazy; and I cannot bear
Uncertainty.

If I lose you I'll die;
But waiting any longer, that would be
The end of me as well.
Too many fears and threats and groans already.
So think it over. When I come back—soon—
I'll take you to the temple: there
Your son awaits me. All turns on your whim:
Do I crown you?
                    Or do away with him?

SCENE EIGHT

ANDROMACHE, CEPHISA

CEPHISA
As I foretold, in spite of all the Greeks
You're still the mistress of your destiny.

ANDROMACHE
But what a destiny! My only choice
Is whether to condemn my child to death.

CEPHISA
One can be over-faithful to one's husband;
Excessive virtue may become a vice.
He'd want you to be happy . . .

54

ANDROMACHE

And want me to set Pyrrhus in his place?

CEPHISA

I know what Hector's son would have you do,
Before the Greeks can do away with him;
And Hector's ghost.

           It has no cause to walk
Or be ashamed his widow's with a king,
And a victorious one, who offers you
The rank bequeathed you by your ancestors,
Who tramples underfoot your conquerors
For all their fury; does not recollect
His father was Achilles; disavows
His father's deeds; undoes them.

ANDROMACHE

Do I have to forget, if Pyrrhus chooses
Not to remember? What must I forget?
Must I forget my husband left unburied
Dragged in dishonour round and round the walls?
Should I forget his father's body, tumbled,
Clutching the altar, blood all over it?
Remember, Cephisa, that evil night
A dawnless nightfall for the Trojan race,
And there see Pyrrhus with his glittering eye,
Under the light of burning palaces
Hacking a pathway through the piled-up dead,
The corpses of my brothers, Pyrrhus
Drenched in their blood but still hellbent on slaughter.
The noise, Cephisa, that the victors made;

55

The noises of the dying
                    choked in flame
Or dying by the blade.
                    Amid these scenes,
Picture Andromache distracted.
                              And so
I first met Pyrrhus. These are the noble deeds
By which he was advanced.
                          And this is he
The husband that you offer.
                          No! I won't.
I will not be accomplice to his crimes;
Let us be his last victims, if he will
And let him feed upon my bitterness.

CEPHISA

Then let us go and watch your child die.
You keep them waiting.
                      Madam, do you tremble?

ANDROMACHE

What dreadful memories you conjure up!
Cephisa,
          must I watch my child die,
And see my Hector killed a second time,
Losing the token of his love for me?
The day he bravely chose to make a sortie
And hunt Achilles—rather, hunt for death—
He had the child brought to him, held him close
'My love' he said—and wiped away my tears—
'I cannot tell what luck I'll have today.
But here's my son, the symbol of my faith;

56

If he lose me, then you must take my place.
And if our marriage has been happy, show
Your love to me by how you love our child.'
And can I watch that dear blood leaking out
And the line die with him?

                Brutal king!
Is he accused of sharing in my crime?
If I do hate you, what way is he guilty,
A co-conspirator?
Does he reproach you for his murdered kin,
Who doesn't even know there's any wrong
Done to him?

            Nonetheless, he's bound to die
Unless I can deflect the blade with which
That tyrant threatens him.

                What, it's in my power
To save him, and I plan to give him up?
Unbearable!

          Let's look for Pyrrhus now.
No Cephisa, find him for me.

CEPHISA
To tell him what?

ANDROMACHE
To tell him that maternal love's so strong . . .
Do you believe he really means to kill?
Can love drive him to such barbarity?

CEPHISA
He'll turn up soon, and in his rage again.

ANDROMACHE

Then promise him . . .

CEPHISA

Promise him what? Your hand?

ANDROMACHE

Am I still free to promise anything?
A husband's ashes! Trojans! Father lost!
My son will live and I shall pay the cost.
Let's go.

CEPHISA

But where?

And what decision have you made?

ANDROMACHE

At Hector's tomb consult with Hector's shade.

ACT FOUR
SCENE ONE

ANDROMACHE, CEPHISA

CEPHISA

O I am certain. Only Hector's spirit
Could work this supernatural change in you;
So Troy will live, and his son will rebuild it.
Pyrrhus has promised. As you heard just now.
A word from you will fetch Astyanax.
Believe his vows: his father, kingdom, friends.
He offers up to you
              And makes you queen
Of him and of his people.
                  Does this sound
The wicked tyrant you do right to hate?
He cares as much as you do for the child.
The hostile plotting of the Kings of Greece
Outrages him.
             He gives the boy his guards
To keep them off, and puts himself at risk.
The temple is prepared, you gave your word;
And we . . .

ANDROMACHE

I shall be there. But first my son . . .

59

CEPHISA

No urgency about that.
                    The main thing is
That from now on he'll not be kept from you
And you can give him all the time you want,
Your hugs need not be rationed.
You'll have the joy of seeing him grow up
Not like a slave who's raised for servitude
But as re-founder of a dynasty.

ANDROMACHE

Cephisa: we are going to say goodbye.

CEPHISA

Dear God, what are you saying?

ANDROMACHE

                    Dear Cephisa,
I can't hide from you what my feelings are.
You've been a loyal friend throughout my troubles;
I thought you understood me.
                    Do you think
That I could cheat a husband who relied
On me to be his deputy?
                    Disturb
The rest of all those noble Trojan dead
So I could sleep the sounder? That's not how
I must keep faith with Hector's memory.
But something must be done to save his son.
When we are married, Pyrrhus must declare
My son is under his protection,

And that will do. I've confidence in him,
For though he's violent, he's no hypocrite,
And what he's promised, he'll perform
                                    and more.
Besides, I can rely upon the Greeks:
Their enmity will get my son a father.
Since I must sacrifice myself, I'll swear
To give myself to Pyrrhus for what's left
To me of life.
                    And he will bind himself
By sacred oaths to guard Astyanax.
The moment that is done, I'll end my life
By my own hand; thus, I'll pay what's due
To Pyrrhus, to my son, and to my Hector
And keep my honour.
And that's my subterfuge. The part
Hector himself commanded.
                                    I go alone
To join my husband and my ancestors.
Cephisa, you must close my eyes for me.

CEPHISA

O don't imagine that I can survive
Without . . .

ANDROMACHE
                Cephisa, I forbid it. I trust you
To guard my only legacy.
                                    If you've lived
For me, then live for Hector's son,
Custodian of Troy's remaining hope.
Imagine, you'll be indispensable
To many kings.

Keep Pyrrhus in his faith
And even—if you have to—talk of me
I will permit it. Let him appreciate
The value of the contract we'll have made.
Tell him, that I was bound to him in life
And all our ancient grudges must be cancelled;
I give my son to show I honour him.
Teach my son the heroes of his race. The deeds
That made them glorious. What they did,
Not what they were. Instruct him every day
About his father. And occasionally
Tell him about his mother.
But Cephisa,
Don't let him dream of vengeance. I have left
A master that he owes obedience to.
Let him be humble. He's of Hector's line,
But all that's left of it. And for what's left,
That last remainder, I'll have sacrificed
At once my life, my grievance and my love.

CEPHISA
(Sobs)

ANDROMACHE
Don't follow me if you can't keep control
Of your emotions. Someone's coming.
Conceal your tears.
And always keep in mind
My fate is in your hands.
Here comes Hermione: let's not wait around,
To hear her violence.

62

SCENE TWO

HERMIONE, CLEONE

CLEONE

I cannot tell you how extraordinary
I find your self-restraint. You hold your tongue
As though this insult didn't hurt your pride,
And bear it mutely.
                    Though I've known you shudder
At the mere mention of Andromache;
And frequently I've seen you quite distraught
If Pyrrhus even looked at her.
                              And now
He's marrying her; he'll give her, with his crown
The vows he made to you.
                          You stand for it
In silence. Not a syllable of complaint.
Madam, your calmness frightens me.
I'd much prefer it if . . .

HERMIONE

Orestes? Have you sent for him?

CLEONE

He's on his way. And shortly you shall see
How eagerly he volunteers himself
Without the smallest hope of recompense;
The sight of you's enough.
                          But here he is.

SCENE THREE

ORESTES, HERMIONE, CLEONE

ORESTES
Lady, is it true.
This once, you wanted me to come and find you?
They said you sent for me: or did they lie
And flatter with false hope:
                                        or finally
I don't repel you?

HERMIONE
I sent for you to ask you if you love me.

ORESTES
If I love . . . haven't I sworn and lied;
Escaped and then come back; praised you and spoken ill;
Despaired and wept: indeed, am weeping still
Does this convince you?
                                        If not, nothing will.

HERMIONE
Avenge me, I'll believe it all.

ORESTES
                                        Then let's go
And set all Greece ablazing, as before;

You will be Helen, Agamemnon I;
We'll put them through the sufferings of Troy,
And be as famous as our fathers were.
Let's go: I'm ready.

HERMIONE
No, let's stay.
I do not mean to be so tolerant,
And glut the insolence of our enemies
By going far away to plot slow vengeance;
To risk all on the fortunes of a war
That might not favour me.
I want Epirus
Plunged into mourning by the time I leave.
If you'll be my avenger, do it now.
Go to the temple, quickly.
There kill . . .

ORESTES
Who?

HERMIONE
Pyrrhus.

ORESTES
Kill Pyrrhus?

HERMIONE
What? Have you lost your nerve?
Run and just hope that I don't call you back;

And don't remind me what I owe to him.
It's not for you to try to justify him.

ORESTES

Me justify him? When I know too well
The way he's treated you?
                                    Vengeance, yes
But let us not be assassins:
                                    let us find
A way to make his downfall clearly justice.
What! As his answer, bring the Greeks his head?
Put on my whole ambassadorial rig
And end my mission with a shoot-out? No!
Let Greece take on the role of judging him
And let him die by due process of law;
Remember he's a king and wears a crown . . .

HERMIONE

It's not enough for you I sentence him?
It's not enough for you, that I've been hurt
And someone has to pay for it? It's not enough
That I'm the prize for bringing down the tyrant?
It's not enough I hate him? And to cap it all
It's not enough for you that I have loved him?
I'll not deny: he knew the ways to stir me;
Was it for love or just to please my father? Well,
Never mind. Just concentrate and fix your mind on this:
Despite my vows so shamefully betrayed,
Despite the way his crimes disgust me, this:
While he's alive I'm liable to forgive him.
Don't trust my anger; till I'm sure he's dead
I might decide to live with him instead.

ORESTES

Then he must die, before you change your mind
And I must . . . what precisely must I do,
Seeing that your rage demands immediate blood?
What's the best way for me to get at him?
I've only just got here, I'm still a stranger
Newly arrived; and you say 'Kill the King!'
And throw the state in uproar; you insist
The King must die; his time of punishment
Must be today, must be this hour, this minute.
The King must die where all his subjects see!
Let me instead find ways to lead him off
Up to the altar, like a sacrificial
Animal.
        I won't procrastinate
I only need to pick the place to act.
When I know where, tonight I shall attack.

HERMIONE

But it's today he'll marry Andromache!
The wedding thrones are waiting in the temple:
My shame is public, and his crimes complete.
Why are you waiting? He's a sitting duck,
Performs the ritual walk alone, unarmed;
His bodyguards have all been given orders
To escort Hector's son. So he's a target
For any one who'd execute my vengeance.
Must you take better care of him than he himself?
Call out the Greeks. Give weapons to my followers.
Alert your friends, mine are prepared already.
He has betrayed me, cheats you, scorns us all.
Their hate already is as fierce as mine;
You give the word and Pyrrhus won't escape;

Just let them act: if you're afraid to lead
Then take the lead from their well-ripened anger:
Come back to me with Pyrrhus' blood on you,
And you'll be welcomed: you can count on it.

ORESTES
Lady, think . . .

HERMIONE
Enough of thinking
All these excuses only make me angry.
I thought I'd found a way to make you
Make me love you: but now it's very plain
You'd rather stand and wail about your love
Than earn mine.
                    Run along
Go somewhere else and boast how you are faithful
And leave the work to me.
                            I've been too soft
And all of you reject me.
                         I shall go
Alone to the temple where they plan the wedding
And where you dare not win my gratitude.
I'll find a way of getting close to him
And rip that heart no other means can move.
And then I'll turn my dagger on myself
And so, despite him, we'll be joined at last.
Though he's betrayed me, in the end it's true
I'd rather die with him than live with you.

ORESTES

That may be so, but I'll prevent you making
That grisly choice. I'll be the one to kill him
And rid you of your enemies.

                    Afterwards

You can reward my service, as you please.

HERMIONE

Then leave your destiny for me to shape
And let your ships prepare for our escape.

SCENE FOUR

HERMIONE, CLEONE

CLEONE

But this will be your ruin. Bear in mind . . .

HERMIONE

Ruined or not, what's on my mind is vengeance.
For all his promises, I don't know for sure
If I can bank on anyone but myself.
He doesn't feel, as I do, Pyrrhus' guilt.
I trust myself to strike; I don't trust him.
What pleasure to pay him out by my own act,
To see his cheating blood upon my hands;
And it would be the peak of satisfaction

69

To come between him and Andromache
As he lies dying. But if Orestes does it,
He's spared the hurt of knowing that I killed him.
Go to Orestes. Tell him to make sure
That Pyrrhus knows he's dying from my hate
And not from any high Affairs of State.
Cleone, darling, run.

                       I need for him to know
As he is dying
                   that I aimed the blow.

CLEONE

I'll do it right away.

SCENE FIVE

PYRRHUS, HERMIONE, PHOENIX

PYRRHUS

You weren't expecting me, and my arrival
Is an intrusion. Madam, I've not come
To try and justify my shabby treatment
Of you by any crooked form of words.
I cannot argue in my own defence
When I've a conscience which will not acquit me.
I'm marrying a Trojan. I admit it;
And I admit that that fidelity
I swear to her was sworn before, to you.

Another man might claim that our betrothal
Arranged between our fathers, there in Troy,
Without consulting us on how we felt,
Was an alliance of expedience
That tied us without love.

                The crucial thing
Is that I had the chance to raise objections
And didn't take it. My ambassador
Accepted the proposals. Far from choosing
To disavow them, I endorsed the plan.
I watched them bring you to Epirus here;
And though by then I'd fallen in the power—
The invincible power—of someone else's eyes
And never knew what your power might have done
If I'd given it a chance; and yet—I didn't cling
To this new feeling, but tried to keep myself
Loyal to you. And so when you arrived,
Received you as a Queen, and up till now
Have hoped fine words would take the place of love.
Love overpowered me. By an ironic twist
Andromache gained a heart that she detested.
Swept up in one another, we are rushing
To sanctify our love, despite ourselves.
I've had my say. Abuse me as the traitor
I know—to my regret—I choose to be.
For me, I won't do anything to stop you
Expressing what you feel. You've every right
To anger. It might ease my conscience too.
Curse me in every way that I deserve
For breach of promise. It's your silences
That I'm afraid of, more than any words
That you can say; because the less you say,
My heart (which sits in judgement on my actions
And hears a thousand witnesses against me)
Condemns me all the more.

HERMIONE
                              I'm glad you're honest
And don't use any verbal trickery
To mitigate your actions. Once decided
To break your solemn oath, you went ahead
As to the manner born.
                              But after all,
Does it seem right that noble conquerors
Should be obliged to keep their promises
Like common people?
                              Besides, you stood to gain
From treachery.
                              You've only come to gloat;
Why else should someone who has won a Trojan
Seek out a Greek, when neither word not duty
Compel him to?
                              First you abandoned me,
Then took me back, then crawled away again.
The wife of Hector, or the child of Helen;
The slave or the princess; you hounded us
Alternately.
                              First Troy put to the torch
To please the Greeks; and now you offer up
A Greek as victim to the son of Hector.
This from a man who always knows his mind
A hero who's not bound by common laws
Like keeping trust.
                              Is it to please the bride
That I must load you with sweet compliments
Like 'perjurer' and 'traitor'?
                              Have you come
To see how badly I am taking it,
And report back and laugh at my distress
While you are fondling her?

                                        Do you need to have
Me march in tears behind her chariot?
                                        No.
Too much enjoyment for a single day.
And don't ask me to find new epithets
To decorate your name, but be content
With those exploits that you're so famous for:
Like Hector's brave old father, put to death
In front of all his family, while your sword
Dug deep to find the last few drops of blood
Left in that withered body;
                                        blood
Flowing in floods to quench the fires of Troy;
Polixena, the girl whose throat you cut
With your fair hand, while even the Greeks who saw
Were outraged by it.
                                        How could one refuse
A man with such a record anything?

                        PYRRHUS
                                        Madam.
I know, too well, my keenness to avenge
The wrongs done Helen, made me go too far
In actions of excessive violence.
The blood I shed is therefore down to you
Or to your family; but I don't complain.
I'll let bygones be bygones.
                                        I'm pleased to note
Your calm towards my new-found happiness
Shows me that it's not culpable.
                                        I thank
Heaven for that fact. I've been too sensitive;
I should have known you better

and myself.
I do you wrong by being apologetic;
If one's not loved, one cannot be unfaithful
And you don't claim you've any hold on me.
I feared I'd hurt you: on the contrary,
It's possible I've done you a good turn:
For our planned marriage was not made in Heaven,
But I was doing what seemed to be my duty
As you submitted to yours;
no real bond
Impelled you to feel any love for me.

HERMIONE

I didn't love you? What do you think I felt?
Princes proposed to me, I turned them down
And followed you to this benighted place
And here I am, for all your double-dealing.
And though the Greeks thought you dishonoured me
I made them hold their tongues.
And waited still
For you to get this thing out of your system.
I reckoned, late or soon, you must remember
Where duty lay, and bring me back your heart.
I loved you, faithless as you are; and how much more
Would I have loved you if you had been true.
And even now, when your damned cruel tongue
Announces cheerfully that I am dead,
I fear the fire's not altogether out.
What needs must be, must be.
If angry Heaven
Has granted someone else the privilege
Of pleasing you—
then let the bells ring out!

Please, don't insist that I must be a witness.
This may be the last time that I talk to you.
Postpone the wedding for one day; do what you please
Tomorrow.
            You don't answer?
                          Damn your eyes,
You're counting every moment spent with me
As wasted. So impatient to get back
To see your Trojan, all that you regret
Is spending time with someone else.
                          Get out.
What's keeping you?
                Not me.
Go swear to her the oaths you swore to me
Blaspheme against the honour of the Gods.
The Gods are just, and they do not forget
That those same vows bound you and me together.
Go to the altar with your turncoat heart.
Run.
        But you haven't heard the last of me.

SCENE SIX

PYRRHUS, PHOENIX

PHOENIX
You heard her, Sir, and cannot just ignore
A castoff lover, looking for revenge.
She has supporters here.
                    And all the Greeks
With whom you quarrel, will take sides with her.
Orestes loves her still . . .

PYRRHUS
                    Andromache
Is waiting for me. Phoenix, guard the child.

ACT FIVE
SCENE ONE

HERMIONE

HERMIONE

Where am I? What have I done? What must I do?
What passion overcomes me? What's the grief
That eats me up? Why am I wandering
At random through this place?

                   Why can't I tell
Whether I love him more than I detest him
Or what I feel?

              How he looked at me
When he gave me my marching orders!
He said 'Goodbye' without the least pretence
Of feeling sad: he didn't try to look,
Even for a moment, as though he pitied me,
Nor could I make him feel the need to try
To squeeze a single solitary tear
From eyes that looked with such tranquility
On my distress. I sighed, and he was silent;
I cried, and Pyrrhus looked at me as if
It hadn't anything to do with him.
And I'm still sorry for him.

                   Even worse,
Coward that I am, I take his part.
I tremble at the blow that waits for him:
I plot revenge but find excuses—

                   No,
I won't give up an atom of my rage
He's dead to me, so let me see him dead.

Now, he rides high; my hate amuses him
As if this storm were just a passing shower,
Blowing itself out in tears.
He thinks of me as weak, irresolute;
As if, when one arm was upraised to strike
The other arm would interpose itself
To save him.
     Pyrrhus thinks
That I'm the soft, good-natured thing I was;
Perhaps he doesn't think like that at all:
Gloating in his temple, doesn't even think
There might be someone else who wants him dead
Or to survive . . .
     The callousness of him,
That leaves me in this low, uncertain state!
Then let Orestes act. For he must die.
He must have seen it coming. He has acted
Deliberately to make me want his death.
To want it?
    Is it me that orders it?
Is death the net result of all my love?
This Prince, whose deeds I thrilled to listen to,
Whom, secretly, I'd chosen for myself,
Even before the marriage was arranged,
Have I crossed all these seas and all these lands
And come so far to make an end of him?
To slaughter, to destroy him?
       Yet before,
Before he dies . . .

SCENE TWO

HERMIONE, CLEONE

HERMIONE

What have I done? What have you come to tell me?
What's Pyrrhus doing?

CLEONE

         He's in the seventh Heaven.
The proudest man alive, the most in love.
I watched him on his way toward the temple,
Where all the ceremony has been prepared,
In a triumphal march, with his new conquest,
His face ablaze with happiness and hope;
Half drunk in his delight in watching her,
Andromache, who walks through cheering crowds,
And brings with her the memory of Troy
Up to the very altars . . .
              She appears
Incapable of either love or hate,
Joyless and uncomplaining.
                She obeys.

HERMIONE

And *him*? Will he go through with this disgrace
To the bitterest end? Did you observe his face
Closely, to look for any sign of doubt
To trouble his sweet plesasure? Did he glance
In this direction? Did he look at you?

79

And when he knew you, had he grace to blush
For his betrayal? Or did me maintain
His poise intact?

CLEONE
He had no eyes to see
Anything. Public Opinion and Security,
And you, have simply vanished from his mind.
He presses forward with his marriage plans
Without a thought of who is following:
Subjects or plotters.
                              He's got his bodyguards
Protecting Hector's son, as if he thought
That no one else was threatened. In command
Is Phoenix. He has had the boy escorted
To a distant fort, one well away from both
The temple and the palace. In his state
Of ecstasy, this is his sole concern.

HERMIONE
The cheat! He'll die.
                              What did Orestes say?

CLEONE
Orestes and his Greeks are in the temple.

HERMIONE
Is he prepared to strike the blow for me?

CLEONE

I don't know.

HERMIONE

You don't know! What then?
Does Orestes mean to let me down as well?

CLEONE

He worships you. But he is in two minds
He's struggling with a thousand different guilts
Torn between love and honour.
                              In Pyrrhus
He sees a lawful king, he sees Achilles;
Sees Pyrrhus himself as worthy some respect.
He fears what Greece may do; fears the whole world
Will turn against him. Most of all he fears
Himself. He wants to bring you Pyrrhus' head
But he's aghast at being an assassin:
That makes him stop. He went into the Temple
Not knowing how he would come out again—
As killer, or as one face in a crowd.

HERMIONE

O he'll take care he doesn't spoil the show!
He'll watch them glory, and not interfere.
I know the kind of guilt that tears at him:
He's scared of dying and that's all he's scared of.
My God! My mother didn't have to say a word
To have the whole of Greece from end to end
In arms for her: and in ten years of war
Some twenty kings, who'd not clapped eyes on her

Died in her quarrel.
                Me, I only claim
A single traitor's death, and charge my lover
To cleanse the wrong that has been done to me;
And I'm the prize for doing what I ask:
I offer him myself. Still he won't act!
Let's go: I understand it's down to me
To see that I have justice. Let the temple ring
With cries of agony. We'll interrupt
This deadly marriage; if they must be joined
It will not be for long.
                Or not at all.
There's such a wild uproar in my mind
I shan't be fussy whom I choose to kill;
Each face I see will seem like Pyrrhus' face
Even Orestes. Obviously I'll die.
At least this way I won't die unavenged
And not alone. Someone will come with me.

SCENE THREE

ORESTES, HERMIONE, CLEONE

ORESTES

It is done!
        Hermione, I've carried out your orders
Pyrrhus is yielding up his crooked ghost
Upon the altar.

HERMIONE
He's already dead?

ORESTES

He's dying; and the Greeks whom he provoked
Have washed away his treason with his blood,
Just as I promised.
        Though privately I feared
The outcome of this grim conspiracy,
I rushed towards the temple with my men;
They scattered through the crowd, and worked their way
Up to the altar. Pyrrhus noticed me;
He didn't turn a hair. My presence even seemed
To make him cockier: Greece herself defied
In the person of the Greek ambassador;
And the Greek delegation gathered there
Just to add colour to his wedding day.
And finally, he lifted up his crown
Triumphantly; turned to Andromache
And placed the diadem upon her head

With his own hands; and said something like this:
'Andromache, I give you here my crown
As token of my faith; rule Epirus,
Rule me.
               I vow to be a father to your son;
I swear it to his mother, call the Gods
To witness; all his enemies be mine;
I hereby recognize him King of Troy.'
The crowd applauded.
                         All except the Greeks
Who only answered him with cries of rage
And fell on him. The traitor was hemmed in
On every side by swords; I couldn't find
A place to strike at him, as our men vied
To have the honour of the *coup de grâce*.
I saw him struggle for a while and try—
All bleeding as he was—to get away
But finally he crumpled on the altar.
The crowd was stunned; I fought my way through them,
Made my way here to reach you and conduct you,
Safe to the port, where soon our friends will come
All covered with the blood I promised you.

HERMIONE

What have they done?

ORESTES
               Forgive their eagerness.
I see that they have somewhat spoiled your vengeance.
You wanted me to get my blow in first,
So that he'd know he died for what he'd done
To you. But it was my example fired them up;

For you alone I led them to the temple,
And you can take the credit for a death
Of which they were the passive instruments;
You gave the thrust.

HERMIONE
Shut your mouth, you killer!
Don't dare to implicate some other person
In the cowardly murder you did by yourself.
Boast to the Greeks about your violence.
Go. You disgust me. I've no part of it.
What have you done, you savage?

What mad fit
Came over you, to end that noble life?
How did you dare to kill him? Cruel mob,
How come your very arms did not refuse
To do the dirty deed? What right had you
To be his judge? Why kill him? For what crime?
What had he done? What was he guilty of?
Who told you to?

ORESTES
O Gods! Didn't you,
Yourself, here, just now, on this spot,
Order his death?

HERMIONE
Then why did you obey
A half-crazed lover? Hadn't you the wit
To look a little deeper in my mind,
And realize I was beside myself

And not responsible for what I said?
And if I really meant it, did you have
To go along? When what you should have done
Was check and recheck with me a hundred times,
And check with me again before you struck
And check again—or, better, keep away.
And why not leave my vengeance up to me?
What brought you to these parts, where no-one wants you?
This is the hateful product of your 'love'.
You had to dump on me the rotten luck
That follows you around.

                Your embassy
Has ruined both of us. That was the thing
That swung him over to Andromache.
Before it, he at least showed some concern
For each of us; and maybe he'd have come
To love me once again—at least pretend to.
Goodbye.

          You go.

               I stay in Epirus.
I wash my hands of Greece, my family
And Sparta and her Empire. It's enough
That they've produced a maniac like you.

SCENE FOUR

ORESTES

ORESTES

What's happening? Was that Hermione?
I shed his blood; for whom did I do that?
She tells me I'm a traitor:
                    she must know;
She tells me that I am a murderer.
Did Pyrrhus die? Orestes, is that me?
I doused the light of reason in my heart,
Muffled the voice of conscience, killed a king
Whom I respected; broke the laws that fix
Duties and rights for kings and diplomats
And how all men should act. And even worse,
My desecration of the altar where
I furiously attacked him; making me
An outcast, an assassin, a blasphemer:
For whom? And why?
                  Because I made a promise
To one who gives me nothing in return;
Who wouldn't look at me, if Pyrrhus lived;
I made her madness mine.
                    And when I'd done
She orders me to bring him back to life;
She loves him; I'm a monster; off she goes
For ever. And she pays me as she goes
With every evil name that I've incurred
Through trying to please her. That is my reward.

87

SCENE FIVE

ORESTES, PYLADES, ORESTES' TROOPS

PYLADES

We have to leave, Sir. Leave the palace now;
For otherwise we'll have to stay for ever.
We hold the gate, we cannot hold it long;
The mob is armed and they are after us;
Andromache gives orders, they obey;
And she is Queen, and we are enemies.
That same Andromache, who struggled so
Against him while he lived, now does for Pyrrhus
All a devoted widow ought to do:
Demanding vengeance for him, upon us
And vengeance too for Hector and for Troy.
Hurry. We mustn't wait till we're surrounded.
Our Greeks will rendezvous: and while the mob
Is at a standstill round Hermione
We have a moment when the path is clear
We safely can evacuate from here.

ORESTES

No, comrades, I go with Hermione.
She has passed sentence: I must not survive.
The crime was mine and I must pay for it.

PYLADES

Forget Hermione. Put her out of mind.
For how much longer are you bound to be

88

The weapon and the target of her hate?
Will you look for some new insult from the dead:
Because she dies, are you obliged to die?

ORESTES

Because she dies? O Gods, what do you mean?

PYLADES

You didn't know?

We met her on the way as we returned,
Running towards the temple, frantically
And quite distracted. She found Pyrrhus there
Carried upon the shoulders of a squad
Of soldiers bent on vengeance.

How this sight
Must have affected her! Then, from the gate,
We saw her with a dagger in her hand
Bend over Pyrrhus, raise her eyes to Heaven,
And stab herself and fall.

ORESTES

Thank you, Heaven.
My misery is more than I dared hope for.
Gods, I admire you for your thoroughness
And endless readiness to torture me.
With true solicitude you've guided me
Up to the very summit of despair;
To amuse yourselves you've brought me crashing down.
And I was born to be the archetype
And model, of a victim of the Gods,
So I can die content, because my fate's
Accomplished.

          Tell me where the lovers are
I have to drown in my blood and in theirs.
I need to see them both as I am dying,
And link three hearts that could not beat in time
When we were living.
               What is this sudden darkness?
Where must I go? Why am I shivering?
What horror grips me?
             I can dimly see . . .
O God, these streams of blood!

PYLADES
Lord Orestes!

ORESTES
What Pyrrhus, is it you I meet again,
My hated rival, can't I get away?
And how did you escape with all those wounds?
Take that! The thrust that I've been saving for you . . .
What now? Hermione's arms embracing you
Have snatched you out of danger. O my Gods,
What ghastly looks she gives me.
                What are these
Demons and serpents that are following her?
Daughters of Hell, have you come here to strike?
The snakes that hiss around your hair, for whom
Are they intended? Your whole retinue,
Have they come here to drag Orestes off
To everlasting night? I yield to you.
But no; back off! And let Hermione
Claw me and rip me: she is good at that,

Better than you. And here's my heart for her
So she can tear it out
                    and chew on it!

PYLADES

He has passed out. And we've run out of time.
This fit gives us a chance to rescue him.
Lift him.
            Look sharp.
                        There's nothing we can do,
If he's still raving mad when he comes to.

TRANSLATOR'S NOTE

The text is that of the 1697 edition. I found the notes of Bernard Lalande, in the Librairie Larousse edition, very helpful.

Evidently I have not tried to produce a close transcription of the original, but have aimed at near-current spoken British English.

I am grateful particularly to Jonathan Miller, for giving me the opportunity—unsought and unexpected—for this attempt, and for his encouragement. I thank those who read the text and suggested emendations: Peter Eyre, Lucy Ellmann (for countless improvements), Marianne Korn (who also made good my want of punctuation), Maurice Whitby for friendly rigour and unstinted pains. They have helped me avoid many blunders and infelicities, but bear no sort of responsibility for the many that doubtless remain.

E.K.

LOVE IN *ANDROMACHE*

An Afterword

Racine's four principals in *Andromache* extend a love triangle into—not a rectangle, but a quivering line of unrequited yearning. Orestes loves his cousin Hermione, who loves (and is promised to) Pyrrhus, who loves his war captive Andromache. If this were a play by Chekhov we would expect the author to complete a geometrical figure by tying the ends of the line together, as happens in say, *The Seagull*. Andromache would then love Orestes. But she doesn't. She breaks the pattern by clinging fiercely to the remembrance of her dead husband Hector and possessively to the life of her small, endangered son Astyanax.

Love? What does *love* mean in this fearsome drama? Not much that is affirmative. Not much to heat the heart of a sentimental spectator. It signifies a passion that amounts to illness, an alternately aching and frantic desire that cannot be slaked. The three characters who love strive to conquer love by straining their will power to its elastic limits. When will power fails, they try bargaining: in eloquent, desperate reasonableness they plead that so much suffering deserves at least a token return. When bargaining proves fruitless, they turn to psychic, self-administered medicine: they condemn themselves, as though to demonstrate that they can step out of their own skins and observe themselves with the eyes of the ones who are disinterestedly loved. As a final ploy, one of them, Pyrrhus, who controls the fate of Astyanax, uses threats to get some of what he wants—marriage to Andromache without her love—but in achieving this restricted success, he ignites a catastrophe the dramatic logic of which dictates that he and Hermione will die while Orestes will descend into madness.

And what does *loved* mean here? Not the ecstasy of glowing with selflessness and basking in another's affection, but a tormenting burden that cannot be shaken off, can only be readjusted to serve as an instrument of convenience or harm. Andromache trades on Pyrrhus' love for her by agreeing to marry him if he swears to adopt and preserve her son. Hermione makes use of Orestes' love for her by dropping hints that she will look on him more favorably if he kills Pyrrhus. Loving, then, means violent soul-diseased jealousy. Being loved can mean indulging a sick spite. Racine was not alone among his contemporaries in taking this view of love as an ailment; Eugène Vinaver cites a famous novel of the time, *Le Grand Cyrus*, in which a character says, "Love is a kind of malady whose venom is contagious."

Among the members of the Racinian quartet two, Hermione and Pyrrhus, love and are also loved, but unreciprocally, discordantly. And fatally. Pyrrhus is slain as the culmination of his wedding ceremony. Over his body Hermione immolates herself on her own knife. Orestes, who opens and closes the play, the one who loves but remains unloved, learns of her death and slumps into an insanity plagued by visions, and then into unconsciousness, like a reminder of the Orestes in Aeschylus' trilogy whom the Furies hounded after he murdered his mother. Andromache, the only one of the four who was an object but not a subject of love's predations, is the only one who evades retribution. Through her marriage to Pyrrhus she becomes queen of the city-state of Epirus and assures the future of her child. Even so, she had a close call. Because Pyrrhus was the son of Achilles, who killed her first husband; because he put the sword to Hector's father and sister; because he received her as his spoils, and marriage to him will be a form of self-sullying, she had determined to kill herself as an escape, but only after he took his oath to save Astyanax. The death of Pyrrhus opens a new and larger escape hatch; it proves her respite and salvation. That seems to be the closing implication of the action, that in the course of it Andromache, who gives the play her name, is spared and blessed because she did not love, or loved only a memory.

As a state of sickness, love festers and turns yet uglier. The play's movements contribute to its ruling paradox of love as hatred. The three doomed love-invalids hate themselves for being overtaken by their weakness. One might almost say they also hate those they love, who have (even unwittingly) made them prisoners of their passions. The anything-but-generous feelings to which they yield seethe below the surface of Racine's exquisite verse, here and there smashing through to erupt in terse commands ("Warn them!"), exclamatory appeals to the gods in the name of justice, assertions ("You love: that's enough"), or questions, such as the explosive sequence from Hermione to Orestes after he reports that his Greek followers have stabbed Pyrrhus at her request: "Why kill him? What had he done? What was he guilty of?"—capped by the play's most startling and celebrated line, "Who told you to?" (*"Qui te l'a dit?"*)

It is strange that Racine's savage drama, like that of his older contemporary, Pierre Corneille, has acquired a reputation among English-speaking people for being decorous, even prim. Perhaps our tepid responses have been swayed too far by the neoclassicists' custom, borrowed from the Greek tragedians, of keeping the bloody deaths out of sight, as well as by their conforming to the constrictions of the three unities, and by the harmonics and counterpoint of the alexandrines, which translators have often flattened into poetasting civilities.

Andromache is a working-out of some of the aftermath

of the Trojan War. As Lionel Abel has remarked, of the four
principals, three are the children of leading performers in the
Homeric myth: Hermione of Helen and Menelaus; Orestes
of Clytemnestra and Agamemnon; Pyrrhus of Deidamia and
Achilles. The lapse of a generation is complicated by the
presence of Andromache, who ought to be ten or more years
older than the other three (unless she was fifteen to twenty
years younger than Hector, in which case that redoubtable
warrior would, during his feats of arms, have been rather
stretched in the sinew). Such a literal consideration doesn't
need to affect the casting: at the first performance the role
was assigned to Racine's mistress, the gorgeous Mlle du
Parc; today she is played as with the others, rather than as an
older *femme fatale*.

Euripides explored with poetic licence some of the
prefigurings, events, and consequences of that war in no
fewer than nine of the nineteen surviving plays attributed to
him *(Iphegeneia in Aulis, Helen, Hecuba, Andromache, The
Trojan Women, Orestes, Electra, Iphigeneia in Tauris,
Rhesus)*. Racine draws his source material from several of
these, and also from *The Iliad*, *The Aeneid*, and Seneca's
Troades, but especially from the Euripidean *Andromache*
and *The Trojan Women*. In *The Trojan Women* the Greeks
hurl Astyanax from the walls of Troy to the rocks below; in
Andromache the heroine has had an illegitimate son by
Pyrrhus, who is now married to Hermione; the child
survives and will become king of Molossia, according to a
prophecy by the goddess Thetis. In his adaptation Racine
dissolves the bastard son and the marriage between Pyrrhus
and Hermione, and revives Astyanax. His second preface to
the published play defends the reincarnation ("the extended
life") of Astyanax on patriotic grounds, following the lead of
Ronsard's *The Franciade*, written 95 years earlier in 1572,
of which Astyanax is the hero. Besides, long before Ronsard

"our old chronicles," says the playwright, made the young
prince the forebear of "our ancient kings" and "the founder
of our monarchy." Astyanax thereby becomes to Louis XIV
what Banquo's son Fleance became to King James of
Scotland and England. The direct line of inheritance
deduced by Racine between the Trojan War and
17th-century France, apocryphal or not, seems intended to
shift the play part way out of myth and part way into history,
possibly in order to encourage the author's contemporaries
to experience it much as the Greeks did Euripides, whose
plays illuminate the deeds, and particularly the misdeeds, of
their ancestors.

In Homer, the *Oresteia*, and Euripides we find hardly
one character who does not behave ignobly, and at times
brutally. The French dramatist reinterprets but far from
softens the outlines of his quartet. (Paul Janet has dubbed
those four a "quadrille," tracing their steps in nothing like a
ballroom exercise, only a dance of death.) Racine's Pyrrhus
and Orestes have been, and still are, killers. His Hermione is
possessed by a jealousy she inflames by reminding herself
that her rival is now a slave and that she was betrothed at the
insistence of her father. Menelaus and the honor of their
house are thus as affronted as she is by Pyrrhus' waverings.
These conclude with a broken oath when he at last marries
Andromache, and with an added insult to Hermione when he
conducts the ceremony with pride and pomp. As for
Racine's Andromache, some commentators have faulted her
(although not as severely as the other three), since she
practices deceit in accepting Pyrrhus and at the same time
meaning to deny herself to him by committing suicide as
soon as he has declared that he will protect Astyanax. While
this is true, she will never need to carry out her secret
resolve; and Racine seems unmistakably to place her in a
more favorable light—plenty of pink, no green—by making

her less self-absorbed than the other three. At first a victim faced with the heartrending choice of disloyalty to the dead Hector or slaughter for her son, she rises to a tremendously enhanced status and escapes a tragic outcome. In the other three characters Racine illuminates a tragic flaw, but they do remain heroic—neurotically heroic, monstrously tragic, and psychically crippled by their past, unenviable in their agonies but covetable as roles.

By the last act Pyrrhus and Andromache have, as Roland Barthes says, broken decisively with the old order, that cycle of reprisals actuated by the revenge that begets more revenge. Pyrrhus has become the substitute father of Astyanax, while Andromache has switched her loyalty from her old to her new husband. These two have tried to abandon and atone for the past, to reposition themselves for the future. Her acceptance of him will help to overcome his infamy as the assassin of her in-laws; his slaying at the hands of Orestes will crown him as a martyr. In contrast, Hermione and Orestes, those hapless cousins, remain trapped in the past and die for it. They have nothing to show for their pains, unless one cynically looks on death and madness as refuges providing the most unarguable surcease.

And yet—offer discerning players the chance to perform either Andromache or Hermione, Orestes or Pyrrhus, and they will almost inevitably go for Hermione and Orestes. This in spite of every actor's understandable preference for parts that siphon off an audience's sympathy. But there are larger and deeper considerations. Larger: Andromache and Pyrrhus disappear before the fifth act gets under way and Andromache is also missing from act two; Hermione may not appear in the first act, but she comes on strong in the first scene of act two and keeps returning until practically the end, while Orestes opens and closes the play and holds the stage once or twice in every act. Deeper: Hermione and

Orestes fight their way through more of a range of emotions than the other two do. In her tirades Hermione ventures into tantrums, fiery sarcasm, gloriously fashioned and lethally aimed barbs. Orestes totters throughout on the brink of the madness from which he recovered only a few months earlier and which will bubble up—at any moment, it seems—to swallow him again. When it does, the Furies' assault on him will be reinforced by a ghost of the scarcely-cold Pyrrhus. Insanity, as every actor knows, is even more rewarding to enact than are intoxication or rage.

But the prime consideration is that the cousins are the two truly tragic roles. Not because they did not get what they wanted, but because, in a perverse fashion, they did. The tragic character wills his or her own disaster, simultaneously wishing and fearing, gazing upward at glints and flashes of hope while sliding downward into the pit—understanding when it is too late that those glittering hopes were no more than the pit's distorting mirror. Hermione will commit suicide, the act Andromache merely contemplated. A suicide need not be tragic; it can be melodramatic, even comic or farcical. But Hermione's comes about because she has made it impossible for herself to survive while Pyrrhus "belongs" to another—to *this* other. Orestes' tragedy results from his frenzied attempts to win any modicum of satisfaction from Hermione at whatever cost to himself.

Hermione's confidante Cleone and Orestes' friend Pylades (who, in one version of the myth, in Euripides' *Orestes*, will marry Orestes' sister and become his brother-in-law) cannot halt the descent; they exist as debating opponents who never win a point, as sounding boards for stratagems concocted out of despair, as the tragic hero's and heroine's more dispassionate selves, even as consciences. But they do not contribute to or ward off the

101

tragic fates, any more than Phoenix can usefully advise his
obsessed pupil Pyrrhus or Cephisa can help Andromache in
her plight. They are incidentals who show that the four
principals act in accord with ungovernable impulses and
forces that are beyond them. Those forces have ordained that
the cousins meet on this unwelcoming landscape of Epirus, a
neutral, featureless setting in the corner of Greece most
distant from Troy. Here they must play out the last episode
in the fall of the house of Atreus, their common ancestor.

Racine was twenty-seven years old when he wrote
Andromache, the third of his twelve plays, but not the last in
which he would investigate the potency of love as a tragic
sickness.

Albert Bermel
New Rochelle, 1988

SELECTED BIBLIOGRAPHY

The Plays in French:

Oevres Complètes, Tome 1, Théâtre et Poésies, ed. Raymond Picard. Paris: Gallimard, Bibliothèque de la Pléiade, 1964. Not the only complete edition, but compact and well annotated.

The Plays in English:

The Complete Plays of Jean Racine, 2 vols. Translated by Samuel Solomon into blank verse. New York: 1967.

Racine: Five Plays. Translated by Kenneth Muir into blank verse. New York: 1960

Andromache and Other Plays. Translated by John Cairncross into blank verse. New York: 1967.

Criticism in English:

Abel, Lionel. *Metatheatre*, p. 16 ff. New York: 1963.

Barthes, Roland. *On Racine*. Tr. Richard Howard. New York: 1964.

Giraudoux, Jean. *Jean Racine*. Tr. P.M. Jones, Cambridge, U.K.: 1938.

Goldmann, Lucien. *The Hidden God*. Tr. Philip Thody. London: 1964.

Knight. R.C., ed. Racine: *Modern Judgements*. London and Nashville: 1969.

Lancaster, H. Carrington. *A History of French Dramatic Literature in the Seventeenth Century*. Baltimore, MD: 1929-42.

Lapp, J.C. *Aspects of Racinian Tragedy*. Toronto and New York: 1964.

Vinaver, Eugène. *Racine and Poetic Tragedy*. Tr. P. Mansell Jones. New York: 1959

Weinberg, B. *The Art of Jean Racine*. Chicago: 1963.